# RICHARD PETTY:
# "The King"

BY MICHAEL TEITELBAUM

T RADITION BOOKS™
EXCELSIOR, MINNESOTA

Published by **Tradition Books™** and distributed to the
school and library market by **The Child's World®**
P.O. Box 326
Chanhassen, MN 55317-0326
800/599-READ
*http://www.childsworld.com*

**Photo Credits**
Cover and title page: Allsport/Steve Swope (left and page 4), David Taylor (right)
AP/Wide World: 9, 10, 11, 25, 26, 27 bottom
Sports Gallery: 6 (Tom Riles); 15 (Joe Robbins); 27 top (Al Messerschmidt)
Matt Silk/Sports Immortals: 28

The following photos are the exclusive property of ISC Publications-Archives, © ISC
Publications. All rights reserved. Used with permission: 13, 16, 17 (all), 19, 20, 21, 23

Book production by Shoreline Publishing Group, LLC
Art direction and design by The Design Lab

**Library of Congress Cataloging-in-Publication Data**

Teitelbaum, Michael.
  Richard Petty, "the King" / by Michael Teitelbaum.
    p. cm. — (The world of NASCAR series)
Summary: A simple biography of the NASCAR driver who is the only driver to have won 200
Winston Cup races. Includes bibliographical references and index.
  ISBN 1-59187-010-0 (lib. bdg. : alk. paper)
  1. Petty, Richard—Juvenile literature. 2. Automobile racing drivers—United States—
Biography—Juvenile literature. [1. Petty, Richard. 2. Automobile racing drivers.] I. Title. II.
Series.
  GV1032.P47 T45 2002
  796.72'092—dc21                                    2002004649

Copyright © 2003 by Tradition Publishing Company, LLC

Printed in the United States of America.

R I C H A R D    P E T T Y

# Table of Contents

I N T R O D U C T I O N

# The King

Three thousand pounds (1,362 kilograms) of gleaming metal tears around a track at 200 miles per hour (322 kilometers per hour). Controlling this speeding machine is a driver with focus, attention, skill, experience, and desire. His talents spell the difference not only between winning and losing, but often, between life and death.

The most famous number in NASCAR history was Richard Petty's 43. Petty won a record 200 races.

Welcome to the no-holds-barred, pedal-to-the-metal world of **NASCAR** auto racing. This high-speed sport is loved by millions. **Stock car** racing is as popular in the United States as any professional, big-league team sport. The driver most beloved by fans during the sport's fifty-year history is Richard Petty.

Today NASCAR (which stands for the National Association for Stock Car Automobile Racing) is watched by millions of fans on television. Its drivers are supported by corporate **sponsors,** and the sport itself has become big business. This was not the case when Richard Petty began driving in 1958.

Back in the early days drivers had to pay for their own cars, maintenance, and crews. In Petty's case, racing has always been a family affair. His father, Lee, began driving race cars in 1947. Today, Richard's son Kyle is a NASCAR driver.

Born to the sport, Richard Petty lived and breathed cars and racing from the time he could walk. Through hard work and constant innovation, he earned his famous nickname: The King.

During his 34-year career, Petty set the standard for skill, determination, and victory. His 200 wins may never be surpassed. Also, his record of seven driving championships has only been equaled once (by the late Dale Earnhardt).

His greatest achievement, though, can't be measured in numbers. Richard Petty is the man most responsible for dramatically changing stock car racing. The sport turned from a romping, friendly day at the track, to a big-money, **super-speedway** sport adored by millions.

Petty's feather-covered cowboy hats are almost as famous as his wide smile.

CHAPTER ONE

# A Family Affair

Richard Lee Petty was born in Level Cross, North Carolina, on July 2, 1937. The Petty family, like most families in that small rural town, didn't have much, but they got by on what they did have. Richard's father, Lee, drove a delivery truck to support his family. His true passion, however, was building and driving race cars.

Lee, who won an impressive 54 NASCAR races during his driving career, began driving in 1947. In NASCAR's first season two years later, races were held on dirt tracks. In Daytona, Florida, drivers raced along the hard, flat sands of the beach. Daytona would one day become the home of stock car racing's most famous event, the Daytona 500. Drivers built and maintained their own cars, with no help from sponsors. The prize money was small, but drivers put in the time and risked their lives on the track for the sheer joy of racing.

Lee Petty built, tested, and maintained his race cars in a modest shop on his property. From an early age, Richard was surrounded by the sights, sounds, and smells of engines, parts, and speeding machines.

As a young boy, Richard competed in bicycle races, usually with his brother Maurice. Nine times out of ten Richard was the winner. When he was old enough, Richard began assisting his father in the shop. He quickly became a skilled mechanic.

On race days, the entire Petty family would head out to the track. Richard and Maurice would sit with their mother, Elizabeth, and cheer while Lee blew past the competition to capture another victory.

By the time Richard reached his teenage years, he had developed not only into a top-notch auto mechanic, but a talented athlete as well. In high school, he starred in foot-

ball, basketball, and baseball. When he graduated high school in 1955, Richard went to work full time for his father. Lee ran the family racing business, known as Petty Enterprises.

As much as Richard loved tinkering with engines, it wasn't long before the desire to get behind the wheel became his growing passion. Lee Petty had different ideas, however. He hoped his son would stick to working on cars and eventually develop into a master mechanic. Lee also

**Maurice, Lee, and Richard Petty formed one of NASCAR's greatest racing families.**

respected Richard, however. When he saw the young man's determination to drive, he struck a deal with his son.

Richard would be allowed to drive, but he would have to wait three years until he was 21 years old. Richard agreed to the deal. He didn't want to get behind the wheel of a stock car without his father's help and approval.

For the next three years Richard devoted himself to Petty Enterprises, working on his father's cars and helping Lee win races. Finally, his 21st birthday came on July 2,

Lee Petty was among early NASCAR's top drivers. He won the first Daytona 500 in 1959.

1958. The next day, Richard Petty slipped behind the wheel of a stock car and took off in his first race.

It was the first baby step in what would turn out to be the greatest career in the history of stock car racing.

## PERSONAL PETTY

**Birthday:** July 2, 1937

**Hometown:** Level Cross, NC

**Height:** 6'2" (1.87 meters)

**Weight:** 180 pounds (81 kilos)

**Wife:** Lynda Owens Petty

**Children:** Kyle Petty
Sharon Petty Farlow
Lisa Petty Luck
Rebecca Petty Moffitt

The future King: Here's Richard Petty in 1959, just starting out on his way to racing immortality.

CHAPTER TWO

# First Laps

ichard Petty drove in his first stock car race on a dirt track in the tiny town of Asheville, North Carolina. He was behind the wheel of his father's 1957 Oldsmobile. His cousin Dale ran his **pit crew.** Petty, the **novice** driver, tried not to think about the fact that he had no previous experience.

From the start, Richard felt comfortable behind the wheel of his car—numbered 43 in honor of his father's number 42. Happy just to be driving, his goal was simply to finish the race and not embarrass himself. He did far more than that. Richard finished in sixth place, only six **laps** behind the winner—an amazing start for a rookie in his first race. Richard was impressed with his performance. He also had the overwhelming realization that he belonged behind the wheel of a speeding stock car.

Richard didn't fair quite as well in his next few races. "I got cocky," he said of his performance in those races. He made many rookie mistakes during his first NASCAR season in 1958, frequently spinning out or crashing his car. But with each mistake he made, young Richard Petty learned more and more about what it took to be a successful driver. With each race, his skills improved.

The 1959 NASCAR season kicked off with the opening of the new Daytona International Speedway. The speedway featured a long 2.5-mile (4-kilometer) track. The track had steeply banked corners. These high corners let the zooming cars maintain top speeds even while turning.

Early NASCAR races were sometimes held on rough dirt tracks, such as this convertible race.

NASCAR had been around for ten years. It was about to grow up, however, moving from dirt tracks to superspeedways. With this growth came faster cars—surpassing 160 miles per hour (257 kilometers per hour). Most importantly, this growth brought a huge increase in the number of passionate fans. The sport was about to explode in popularity. The stage was set for a new superstar to emerge in this newer, faster, world of bigger stakes, and Richard Petty was just the man to step into that role.

Excited to participate in the first Daytona 500, Richard ran into engine trouble and had to leave the race after only eight laps. Lee Petty, however, NASCAR's top driver at the time, won the first Daytona 500 that day.

Richard's driving continued to improve throughout the 1959 season. Lee won his second consecutive NASCAR driving championship that year, while Richard was voted NASCAR's Rookie of the Year.

Another major event took place in the life of Richard Petty in 1959. He married Lynda Owens. The following year the first

of the couple's four children was born. Kyle Petty arrived in

June. No one knew it at the time, but Kyle would one day

continue Lee and Richard's NASCAR legacy.

The 1960 racing season brought Richard Petty his first

NASCAR victory. After finishing a very respectable third in

the season-opening Daytona 500 (Lee finished fourth), Richard

won a 100-mile (169-kilometer) race in Charlotte, North

Carolina. It wasn't a major race, but Richard was happy to get

**Since 1959, the Daytona International Speedway has been the home of NASCAR's most important race, the Daytona 500.**

that first victory under his belt. He won two additional races

that year and finished second overall in the NASCAR driver

championship standings. Richard Petty was on his way.

The following year was a bad one for the Petty family. At

the 1961 Daytona 500, both Richard and Lee suffered major

crashes. Although Richard managed to escape serious injury,

Lee was not as fortunate. His severe leg injury required several

operations. He competed in a few more races over the next cou-

ple of years, but the injury ended his driving career.

Lee Petty retired from driving in 1964, a three-time

NASCAR champion, with a record 54 victories. NASCAR's top

driver had stepped down. His son was about to fill his shoes and

carry the family name to even greater heights.

Though Petty's cars were a far cry from today's sleek
models, he steered these big machines to victory after
victory.

# THE BIRTH OF NASCAR

Stock car racing was a simple recreational sport in the 1940s, particularly in southern and rural America. Informal races on dirt tracks held among friends were the norm when Lee Petty began racing in 1947.

A group of drivers, race promoters, and car owners formed NASCAR in 1948. The organization was created to ensure that honesty and a high level of quality would be the standard for stock racing in the United States. Rules were written to make sure the competitions were fairly staged. Prize money for winners was guaranteed.

The idea for a governing organization for stock car racing came from William France, a race promoter and driver. France believed that stock car racing would one day grow into a major spectator sport. He felt the need for an association to keep it focused and honestly run. The group also would prepare for the expansion he was sure would one day come.

Thanks to Richard Petty, among others, William France's vision has become the hugely popular NASCAR we know today.

Up and over! Lee Petty (42) goes flying during a terrible wreck that ended Lee's driving career in the 1961 Daytona 500.

C H A P T E R   T H R E E

# Pulling Away from the Pack

In 1962, Richard Petty started his climb to the top of the sport of stock car racing. He won nine races that year and finished second in the overall driver championship standings behind veteran Joe Weatherly. The next year Richard racked up 14 victories and again ended up second behind Weatherly.

As the 1964 season began, stock car racing underwent some changes. Faster cars were introduced: vehicles that topped 170 miles per hour (274 kilometers per hour). Sponsorship of drivers and racing teams also increased. Often those sponsors were the car manufacturers, allowing for the latest technical advances to appear quickly. The retirement of Lee Petty and others opened the door for new young stars.

Richard Petty captured his first Daytona 500 victory in 1964. He won the race by a full lap over the second-place finisher. Richard also set a record in the event with an average speed of 154.3 miles per hour (248.3 kilometers per hour). That season ended with Richard's first driving championship. His skill and knowledge improved and the cars he drove were consistently among the best maintained on the track, thanks to his team at Petty Enterprises. But Richard's success was not without some controversy.

Petty Enterprises used a new, more powerful engine designed by Chrysler, called the **hemispherical** or "hemi" engine. The engine was legal. NASCAR, however, felt that the

**Richard Petty won his first Daytona 500 in 1964, beginning his domination of that important race.**

hemi engine gave drivers an unfair advantage. It banned the
hemi from NASCAR racing.

Richard Petty boycotted the start of the 1965 season in
protest, and spent most of the year **drag racing,** rather than
stock car racing. Midway through the 1965 season, NASCAR
decided to allow hemi engines in its competitions. Richard
returned to stock car racing, his first love, to participate in 14
races. He won five of them.

The 1966 season began with another victory in the Daytona

In 1965, Petty's powerful Chrysler "hemi" engine was
declared illegal by NASCAR, but was later allowed in
races.

## PETTY FIRSTS

As the most successful driver in stock car history, Richard Petty ranks first in many categories. Here are some of the categories in which he leads in NASCAR Winston Cup career standings:

All-time wins: 200

Races started: 1,184

Top five finishes: 555

Top ten finishes: 712

Pole positions: 126

Laps completed: 307,836

Laps led: 52,194

Races led: 599

Consecutive races won: 10

First to repeat as winner of the Daytona 500

At the 1966 Daytona 500, Petty (43) found himself in a familiar spot—among the leaders. He went on to win the race.

500, as Richard broke his previous record, averaging over 160 miles per hour (257 kilometers per hour). By the end of that year he had captured eight more races, bringing his total to 49. He was closing in on his father's career record of 54 NASCAR victories. The following year, Richard would shatter that record on his way to the greatest single season in NASCAR history.

Oddly enough, Richard began his astounding 1967 season with a loss at Daytona. But before the year ended he would go on to win an unprecedented 27 races, a record that still stands and may never be broken. His 27 victories came in only 48 races, and included an amazing 10 wins in a row. Twenty-seven wins is a respectable total for a career. In 1967, Richard Petty did it in a single season.

It was during that season that Richard earned the nickname that has stuck with him. "The King," as he came to be known, won the NASCAR championship in 1967 by the widest margin in history, and firmly established himself as stock car racing's greatest driver.

Petty's trophy-filled 1967 season remains the greatest ever by a NASCAR driver. He won an amazing 27 races, including 10 in a row.

C H A P T E R   F O U R

# The King's Reign

Richard Petty would never again reach the heights he scaled in 1967. It would have been unrealistic to expect anyone to repeat his mind-boggling achievements of that year. But until his retirement in 1992, Richard would continue to dominate the sport of stock car racing as it grew and changed.

The 1970s saw television alter the world of stock car racing. ABC Sports agreed to televise nine NASCAR races each season, bringing the sport to a huge national audience. Sponsorship of the entire sport and individual driving teams also expanded.

Beginning in 1971 the NASCAR championship was called the Winston Cup. It was named for the company that sponsored it. In 1972, Richard Petty signed the biggest sponsorship

deal in racing history with the STP company. STP is a major a producer of motor oil and **additives.** The STP logo now appeared on Richard's cars and helmets, and he soon became well known to a national TV audience through his commercials for the company.

Back on the track, cars were roaring along at speeds of 200 miles per hour (322 kilometers per hour). By the end of the 1970s, Richard had captured his seventh and final Winston Cup championship and his sixth Daytona 500 victory.

In the 1980s, Richard's driving career began to wind down, although there were still several milestones to be passed. In 1981, he opened the season with his seventh and final Daytona 500 crown. On July 4, 1984, Richard Petty won the Firecracker

With a little help from his friends: Petty gives his pit crew a lift to Victory Lane after a win in a 1977 race.

400 to notch his 200th victory. He won in front of a packed speedway crowd in Daytona that included President Ronald Reagan. This would be Richard's final NASCAR triumph, but his 200 wins remain almost twice as many as any other driver in history.

Richard was lucky to walk away from a horrifying accident in 1988. That incident started him thinking about retirement. The following year at Richmond he failed to **qualify** for the first time in his career. By 1991, he knew that it was time to step down. He announced that 1992 would be his final year. That season he embarked on the "Richard Petty Fan Appreciation Tour," and received long and loud standing ovations at every speedway in which he appeared.

The last checkered flag: Petty zooms across the finish line to win his 200th—and final—NASCAR race, the 1984 Firecracker 400.

In 1997, Richard was enshrined in the National Motorsports Press Association's Hall of Fame in Darlington, South Carolina, joining his father Lee in this great honor. At the induction ceremonies that day, Richard said, "This is the 50th anniversary of Petty racing, so this honor really tops off those 50 years."

Today, Richard's son, Kyle, continues the family driving tradition, behind the wheel of Petty Enterprises' stock cars. Richard still heads Petty Enterprises and directs two NASCAR teams. But for anybody who has ever thrilled to the high speed excitement of NASCAR racing, Richard Petty will always be The King.

Though Richard has waved goodbye to racing, his son Kyle (top) keeps the family engines humming.

# CAREER HIGHLIGHTS

Here are some of the biggest and most important achievements in Richard Petty's amazing career:

- 200 Career NASCAR Winston Cup victories

- Seven-time NASCAR Winston Cup Champion (1964, 1967, 1971, 1972, 1974, 1975, 1979)

- Seven Daytona 500 victories (1964, 1966, 1971, 1973, 1974, 1979, 1981)

- 27 victories in one season (1967)

- Entered in 1,185 races in his NASCAR Winston Cup career

- Competed in 513 consecutive NASCAR Winston Cup races from 1971 to 1989

- Winston Cup Rookie of the Year 1959

- 1971 Driver of the Year.

- Became the sport's first million-dollar driver after the Dixie 500 in 1971

- National Motorsports Press Association (NMPA) Driver of the Year in 1974 and 1975

- Received U.S. Medal of Freedom, highest civilian award in 1992

- First victory as a car owner in 1996 in the Dura Lube 500 at Phoenix with Bobby Hamilton

- Inducted into the International Motorsports Hall of Fame in 1997

Petty wore this racing suit during the 1991 season. Just like their cars, racers are also covered with their sponsors' logos.

# RICHARD PETTY'S LIFE

**1937**    Richard born July 2, 1937

**1947**    Lee Petty begins racing

**1948**    NASCAR formed to promote stock car racing and ensure rules and safety

**1949**    Lee becomes full-time driver and Richard joins his father's pit crew

**1955**    Richard graduates from high school and goes to work for Petty Enterprises full time

**1958**    Drives in his first race

**1959**    Marries Lynda Owens

**1960**    Wins his first race; first child, Kyle, is born

**1964**    Wins his first driving championship and his first Daytona 500

**1967**    Wins a record-setting 27 races in the greatest season any NASCAR driver has ever had

**1979**    Wins his seventh and final driving championship

**1984**    Wins his record-setting 200th race

**1992**    Retires from driving

**1997**    Elected to the National Motorsports Press Association's Hall of Fame

# GLOSSARY

**additives**—Chemicals added to gasoline to give it better performance or make it burn more cleanly

**drag racing**—a race of short distance using specially designed cars built for quick bursts of speed.

**hemispherical**—shaped like half of a sphere

**laps**—a number of complete circles around the track

**NASCAR**—stands for National Association for Stock Car Automobile Racing

**novice**—someone who is new to an occupation

**pit crew**—people who service a race car during a race, putting in fuel, changing tires, and aiding the driver

**pole positions**—first position when beginning a race.

**qualify**—to finish within the top group of racers during a preliminary race in order to enter the main race

**sponsors**—people or companies who put up the money to help a NASCAR team operate

**stock car**—a car very similar to a standard car released for consumer purchase, but with improvements made for racing

**superspeedway**—type of race track with high, banked turns and long straightaways; usually an oval shape of at least 2 miles (3.2 kilometers) long

# FOR MORE INFORMATION ABOUT RICHARD PETTY

## Books

Center, Bill. *Ultimate Stock Car.* New York: Dorling Kindersley, 2000.

Frankl, Ron. *Richard Petty.* Broomall, Penn.: Chelsea House, 1996.

Libby, Bill with Richard Petty. *King Richard: The Richard Petty Story.* New York: Doubleday, 1977.

Owens, Thomas S., and Diana Star Helmer. *NASCAR.* New York: Twenty-First Century Books, 2000.

## Web Sites

### Official Site of Petty Enterprises
*http://www.pettyracing.com*
The site contains the Petty's complete racing records. You can also see how Richard Petty's team's cars are doing in NASCAR races.

### NASCAR's Official Site
*http://www.nascar.com*
Official site of NASCAR. Check up on race results, read biographies of all the drivers, and check the racing schedule. The site often hosts live chat sessions with drivers that you can contribute to.

# INDEX

# ABOUT THE AUTHOR

Michael Teitelbaum has been a writer and editor of children's books and magazines for more than twenty years. He was editor of *Little League Magazine For Kids,* the author of a two-volume encyclopedia on the Baseball Hall of Fame, and the writer/project editor of *Breaking Barriers; In Sports, In Life,* a character education program based on the life of Jackie Robinson. Michael recently completed a book titled *Great Moments in Women's Sports.*